LIVERPOOL
IN THE 1950s

ROBERT F. EDWARDS

The History Press

Dedicated to the memory of
Johnny Lockhart,
1922-1992

Johnny Lockhart's daughter, Marie Colette, is pictured in this 1957 photograph looking through the window of the family home in Somerton Street, Wavertree, whilst her Dad captures the snow-covered scene outside.

First published 2013

The History Press
The Mill, Brimscombe Port
Stroud, Gloucestershire, GL5 2QG
www.thehistorypress.co.uk

© Robert F. Edwards, 2013

The right of Robert F. Edwards to be identified as the Author
of this work has been asserted in accordance with the
Copyrights, Designs and Patents Act 1988.

British Library Cataloguing in Publication Data.
A catalogue record for this book is available from the British Library.

ISBN 978 0 7524 8788 5

Typesetting and origination by The History Press
Printed and bound in Great Britain by
Marston Book Services Ltd, Oxfordshire

CONTENTS

ACKNOWLEDGEMENTS

I would like to thank Liverpool Records Office for allowing photographs from their archive to be reproduced in this publication.

Grateful thanks also to the following people who have made photographs available: Brian Starkey and Liverpool City Police (www.liverpoolcitypolice.co.uk); Kathleen Faulkner, for her late father Johnny Lockhart's photographs; Stewart O'Reilly; George Rimmer; Graham Newall; Paul Seaton, creator of the Woolworths virtual museum website (www.woolworthsmuseum.co.uk). Thanks also to Gerard Fagan for his help and support, and to Michael Galloway for his help in proof reading.

INTRODUCTION

You won't keep us down
Old Liverpool Town,
Not wars or destruction
Or slums all around,
Like a Phoenix she'll rise
Her people will shout,
We'll be here for forever
Or at least thereabouts.

The city of Liverpool has a story to tell, having emerged victorious – but not unscathed – from the Second World War. Living in Liverpool 5, close to the docks, my mother and her sister spent many a sleepless night during the blitz of May 1941, when heavy and sustained bombing by the Germans caused extensive damage to Liverpool and Bootle, as well as our neighbours on the Wirral. They survived trips to and from the air-raid shelter, often returning to the streets where they lived only to find that a neighbour's house or even a whole street nearby had been totally destroyed. Yet even in the face of such disasters, many would still pick their way through the rubble to go to work the next day. My mother attended a job interview at the then fairly prestigious Kardomah Café in the Derby Square area of the city and got the job; the following morning she arrived for her first day at work to find that her new place of employment had been reduced to rubble and wasteland.

During the Second World War, around 3,875 people died in Liverpool, and more than 10,000 homes were destroyed by enemy action. Added to this were the thousands of people seriously injured and the devastation bombing raids wreaked on the city centre and its buildings. It is remarkable then, given all of these circumstances, that following the war the people of Liverpool simply dusted themselves down and started all over again. A massive rebuilding programme began in 1945, which, out of necessity, required the demolition of damaged and unsafe properties. Liverpool Council had previously planned new housing after the First World War on plots of land they had purchased on the outskirts of the city prior to 1939, but the war with Germany put an end to any building work taking place at the time. Fortunately, work on purpose-built towns – like Speke – resumed again after the war, when there was still a desperate need for decent housing.

Perhaps because of the suffering of many throughout the Second World War, or maybe just because some semblance of normality had returned to people's lives, the late 1940s and early '50s produced a baby boom. Some of these youngsters would later, as teenagers, reshape the city's music scene forever, amongst them musicians like Bill Haley and the Beatles.

The 1950s was a decade of renewed hope and a return towards normality – sweet rationing ended in May 1953 and sugar rationing in September 1953, however, the end to food rationing did not come to pass until 4 July 1954, with meat being the last product to become freely available.

The City Council was striding forward with its plans to build new homes but, unfortunately, many people were moved from the communities they had known for decades either out of the city or into faceless modern blocks of flats which began to spring up, American style, in many areas. Over sixty tower blocks were built in the city between 1956 and 1974, providing more than 5,500 homes.

This book features pictures from the Liverpool Record Office City Engineers collection and some previously unpublished photographs by Liverpool photographer Johnny Lockhart, who was born in Liverpool in 1922. He was an avid photographer who enjoyed taking pictures not only of Liverpool's famous and grand city centre buildings, but also of the streets and places where the ordinary folk of Liverpool lived, worked and played.

So, whether you're a Liverpool resident, a visitor, or just curious, join me as we take a nostalgic trip down memory lane to 'Liverpool in the 1950s'.

Robert F. Edwards, 2013

1

THE OVERHEAD RAILWAY AND ITS LINKS WITH BOOTLE

Let's buy a ticket
To ride on the train,
That shelters the Dockers
Who walk in the rain,
That takes us to work
Or on a day out,
To see the big ships
Coming in, sailing out.

The Second World War had ended and in Liverpool it was all change, new council housing was built in Netherton, Speke and Kirkby, while building work that had been halted by Hitler had begun again. One of the more seriously damaged areas of the city was Bootle and it would take a lot longer for that area to recover. The Liverpool Overhead Railway and Liverpool Tramways Company closure in the 1950s also affected Liverpool's links with Bootle.

The Liverpool Overhead Railway, known as the 'Dockers umbrella', was opened on 4 February 1893 by the Leader of the Opposition, the Marquis of Salisbury. It ran from Alexandra Dock to Herculaneum Dock, a distance of six miles. To begin with there were only eleven stations along the route, but because the system was barely used after working hours it was decided to extend the line to encourage the general public to utilise it.

SEE THE DOX!

When in LIVERPOOL
do not fail to see the
WONDERFUL DOCKS
and GIGANTIC LINERS

Permits
to view
LINERS
issued at
Booking
Offices,
PIER HEAD
or
JAMES ST.
STATIONS

ROUND TRIP FARE

9D.
THIRD CLASS

1/-
FIRST CLASS

13 MILES

Special
Arrangements
made for
large parties.

Apply—
MANAGER,
31 James St.,
LIVERPOOL

CHILDREN UNDER 16 HALF PRICE

C. Tinling & Co., Ltd., Printers, Liverpool, London and Prescot.

The Overhead Railway was advertised by the City Council as a tourist attraction, inviting people to ride the railway and view the miles of docks along Liverpool's waterfront. The line was extended northwards to Seaforth Sands in April 1894, and then southwards from Herculaneum Dock to Dingle – this extension opened on 21 December 1896. Dingle was the line's only underground station and was located on Park Road.

Finally, a northward extension was connected to the Lancashire and Yorkshire Railway's North Mersey Branch in the summer of 1905. The Lancashire and Yorkshire Railway ran some of its own specially built trains on the line, in particular during race meetings at Aintree Racecourse. This photograph, taken in 1956, shows the Overhead Railway toward the Strand and Goree.

The railway was carried mainly on iron viaducts, with a corrugated iron decking. It was vulnerable to corrosion, especially as the steam-operated Docks Railway ran beneath some sections of the line. During surveys, it was discovered that expensive repairs would be required to ensure the line's long-term survival – it was estimated that the repairs would cost £2 million.

The Liverpool Overhead Railway Company could not afford the cost of repairs and looked to both Liverpool City Council and the Mersey Docks and Harbour Board for financial assistance, but this was not forthcoming. As a result, the company had no option but to go into voluntary liquidation, and, despite public protest, the line was closed on the evening of 30 December 1956.

The two final trains were filled to capacity with well-wishers and employees of the company. They each left either end of the line, apparently marking the closure with a loud bang as they passed each other. The trains were replaced by the number 1 bus service operated by Liverpool Corporation Passenger Transport, which could not compete with its predecessor's much faster service, and was continually caught up in traffic along the busy Dock Road.

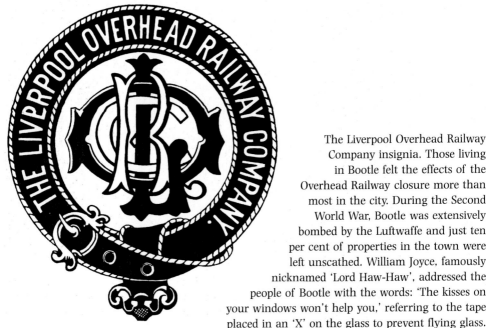

The Liverpool Overhead Railway Company insignia. Those living in Bootle felt the effects of the Overhead Railway closure more than most in the city. During the Second World War, Bootle was extensively bombed by the Luftwaffe and just ten per cent of properties in the town were left unscathed. William Joyce, famously nicknamed 'Lord Haw-Haw', addressed the people of Bootle with the words: 'The kisses on your windows won't help you,' referring to the tape placed in an 'X' on the glass to prevent flying glass.

Bootle was a prime target for the Luftwaffe and damaged street scenes – like this one of 43 Bianca Street – were, regrettably, not unusual. Many of Bootle's factories and industries were affected, forcing residents to travel out of the area for work.

Stanley Road, Bootle, showing a section that was demolished in preparation for the New Strand Shopping Centre development. Because of the extensive damage to property, it was many years before the town started to return to any semblance of normality. In fact, it would not be until the 1960s that the town would benefit from new shops and offices, with the completion of the New Strand Shopping Centre.

Bootle did, however, see new developments take place in the Netherton area, situated in the far south of the Sefton borough, and north east of the centre of Bootle. The Netherton estate was built on the fringes of the Sefton and the road out to Ormskirk and Skelmersdale. This photograph shows the Litherland roundabout on the road out to Netherton.

This photograph shows the Knowsley Road area of Liverpool. Some of the famous names to have been born in Bootle include footballers Jamie Carragher and Steve McManaman, singer and actor Tom O'Connor, and Crissy Rock, the well-known comedian and star of *Ladybird, Ladybird*.

Derby Road, seen here on 6 April 1951, is a route many Bootle residents would travel on a daily basis either to reach the city centre or one of the many factories or dock estates in this heavily industrialised area. The docks continued to be the main source of employment for many Liverpool men, although the work was not regular and men would have to turn up on the day and stand in the 'Dockers Pen', hoping to be picked to work.

On 25 January 1953, the *Empress of Canada* was in Gladstone Dock when a fire was discovered on board by a Mr Halliday at a quarter past four in the afternoon. He immediately sent a man ashore to call the fire brigade. By twenty past six that evening there were thirty pumps in attendance. The ship eventually toppled over onto her side in the dock and burnt out. She was later sent to a breaker's yard in Genoa.

2

SCOTLAND ROAD AND EVERTON DISTRICTS

The wet cobbled streets
And the sound of the docks,
The one o'clock gun
And the holes in our socks,
The games that we played
Where the houses once stood,
All make up memories of
A Liverpool childhood.

I was born in Walton Hospital in the 1950s and, at that time, my family lived in one of the last Athol Street properties scheduled for demolition. They were known locally as 'up the step' houses and were similar to those pictured here, which were also part of the slum clearance programme. My arrival prompted the council, with a little push from the local GP, to re-house my family, so, within weeks of my birth, we moved up the road to one of the new flats that had been constructed post-war to meet the needs of the slum clearance programme.

Athol Street and The Falstaff public house, with an area of waste ground to the right. Logan Towers was later built on this site. Growing up here was a big adventure for small boys – there were a lot of derelict properties known to us youngsters as 'bombies' (bombed houses) and lots of wasteland to play on, which we referred to as 'ollers' or 'hollers'. In later years I learned that this term was derived from 'hollow', i.e. the hollow or crater left in the ground by a bomb or parachute mine.

Athol Street is one of the many streets that run from Scotland Road and the author attended both primary and secondary school in Liverpool 5. In Athol Street was the unusually named St James-the-Less Primary School – known as 'Little Jimmies'. Pictured here is a class photograph taken in 1959. The school adjoined the old Liverpool City Police bridewell and was surrounded on its other sides by St Pius X Roman Catholic School.

This photograph was taken around 1959 at St James-the-Less and belongs to former pupil Stewart O'Reilly. This part of Liverpool was predominantly Catholic and had some of the most beautiful and ornate Catholic churches in the city, including St Anthony's in Scotland Road, St Gerard Majella in Boundary Street, St Alphonsus in Great Mersey Street, and St Sylvester's in Sylvester Street. The Church of England St James-the-Less stood on the corner of Stanley Road and Cranmer Street and was bombed in 1941.

Here pupils demonstrate their artistic abilities. Note the times table charts on the wall – an intrinsic part of learning in those days; every pupil was expected to memorise and recite them to the whole class as and when asked to do so. St James-the-Less School closed in 1967, with the pupils being moved to Our Lady and St Nicholas Church of England School in Blenheim Street.

Athol Street ran parallel with Boundary Street, running from Scotland Road down toward the docks. All of these streets were connected to the Dock Road by a system of bridges over the Leeds and Liverpool Canal, a source of entertainment and danger for local children. The canal runs parallel with Vauxhall and Commercial Roads and then down past the Tate & Lyle sugar refinery near Burlington Street Bridge.

The canal was particularly popular with local children. The Tate & Lyle sugar refinery discharged hot water into it at this point as a result of the 'sugar manufacturing process'. The temperature of the water naturally made this section ideal to swim in, and it was known locally as the 'hotties' or 'scaldies'. Unfortunately, it was also responsible for the deaths of a number of children who drowned here.

The practice of swimming in the canal dated back many years and was still happening in the late 1950s when I was a child. This photograph shows one of the 'Burlington Street bridge boys' – also known as the 'water rats' – ready to take a dip. With its tenement blocks in Burlington Street and Eldon Street this was an extremely densely populated area of Vauxhall, but with a community spirit you would find hard to match anywhere.

Everybody knew everybody else in Vauxhall and the kids could play on the streets without any fear of harm. Someone would always walk you home when playtime finished, even if you only lived two streets away, and, best of all, there were lots of small shops where you could buy a halfpenny- or penny-worth of sweets. This photograph shows the tenements in Burlington Street.

This photograph was taken looking along Vauxhall Road from Tatlock Street on 30 October 1951, with St Martin's Cottages in the background. The term 'Cottages' was used very loosely indeed as can be seen from the photographs of Ashfield Cottages (opposite) in 1955. They were in Ashfield Street, which was located between Athol Street and Sylvester Street, seen on the right of the photograph.

Opposite, above & below: The need for modern housing is evident in these two photographs. Residents were forced to live in extremely cramped conditions – notice the proximity of the toilet to the cooker, which was situated in the same room that the occupants lived in. Ashfield Cottages were erected in 1871 by the 'Liverpool Labourers Dwelling Company'. The basement areas were bricked up in the nineteenth century, having been found insanitary, and the buildings were earmarked for demolition in 1955.

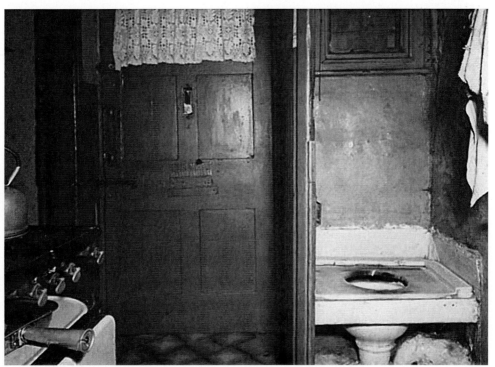

It was only the intervention of MP David Logan, who asked questions in the House of Commons, that brought about the eventual closure of these tenements. However, their demolition resulted in many of the residents being moved out to areas such as Netherton and Norris Green, and was the beginning of the break-up of the Scotland Road area community.

The area, however, remained industrial, particularly over the bridge toward the docks. It was especially hard for those residents who still worked in the Vauxhall area but had been moved to new homes outside the city; the working day was already long and travelling made it longer. This is Bath Street in 1956.

Tate & Lyle were one of the largest employers in the Vauxhall area during the 1950s. Despite the demolition of older properties, new flats had been built in parts of the Scotland Road area, with plans to build even more, including high-rise blocks in Everton. Thus the community was still kept alive, as evidenced by the thriving shopping area of Great Homer Street and Paddy's Market.

Paddy's Market was a fixture in Liverpool for almost 150 years and was home to the fruit and vegetable wholesale market. It was first opened as St Martin's Market on the long-gone Banastre Street in 1862, selling second-hand goods as well as a wide variety of other products. It was situated at the end of Great Homer Street, near the city centre, and was open from 5 a.m. till late afternoon five and a half days a week. Its traders sold fruit and vegetables from all over the world.

Many companies operated out of the market, including the firm of James Rimmer. His grandson, George Rimmer, recalled that in 1918 'at the end of World War One, my grandfather came out of the army and borrowed £20 from his uncle to purchase a pony and cart to go into the wholesale fruit and vegetable trade.'

Later on, prior to the Second World War, motorized vehicles were coming into their own and James Rimmer started buying lorries, including T-type Fords and Bedfords. He ran both means of transport (lorries and horse-drawn carts) until around 1959, when the last team of horses were retired.

Following the Second World War, there was little left of the original market apart from the external walls, and it was eventually relocated to a new purpose-built market on Great Homer Street. Great Homer Street runs parallel with its famous neighbour, Scotland Road. The constant bombardment of the city by bombs and parachute mines took its toll and even buildings that were not hit were still shaken to their foundations during the constant nights of blitzing by German bombers.

The city council were forced to take remedial action to prevent the buildings – many of them occupied homes – from falling down around their occupants. This City Engineers photograph shows the rear of numbers 30-42 Anderson Street, with supports in place to prevent collapse.

Great Homer Street – or 'Greaty', as we knew it – was a place of wonderment to me as a toddler, holding on to my Mother's hand as we wandered along past the myriad of shops. You could buy anything in Greaty, from fish and meat, cakes and biscuits, to pots and pans and all manner of household goods. There were chandlers selling 'Aunt Sally', a disinfectant that, when mixed with a little water, made the best liquid for blowing bubbles.

Numbers 112a-114 Great Homer Street at Rose Vale in 1955, showing Duffy's store. They sold everything from yard brushes to cast-iron frying pans, pegs and washing lines. They also sold galvanised tin baths – which they had hanging outside – and washing blue, sugar soap, ceiling white and scrubbing brushes, all displayed in big enamel buckets inside, which always smelled of paraffin and candles.

Numbers 248 to 250 Great Homer in 1959. Notice the Evangelical church, which was accessed from Potter Street. S. Gordon & Co. Ltd sold cold meats and grocery items. Next door was Lewis's; they sold everything from cigarettes and newspapers to nylons and sweets. As a child my memory of Great Homer Street is of a street lined with shops on both sides, many displaying their wares both inside and outside the premises. Goods seemed plentiful; money, however, was not.

For many, the most important shops of all were the pawn shops. Wives and mothers could be seen entering these shops on a Monday morning with brown paper parcels containing their husband's Sunday suit and perhaps his best overcoat to be 'pledged' in order to get enough money together to put food on the table until Friday, when he got paid. They would then return to the shop and the items redeemed for the weekend, only to go through the same cycle again the following Monday.

Rationing continued after the end of the war. In fact, it became stricter after the war ended than during the hostilities. Bread, which was not rationed during the war, was rationed from 1946 and potato rationing began in 1947.

Butcher's shops became popular again when rationing stopped on 4 July 1954, with the lifting of purchasing restrictions on meat and bacon. I was lucky enough to be born not long before rationing stopped, and therefore never experienced the hardship it caused.

Here we see Great Homer and Roscommon Streets; these buildings would rapidly disappear as the bulldozers moved in and most of the shops and houses where demolished. Properties in the Kirkdale and Everton Valley areas would also be demolished to make way for new buildings.

The Derby Arms public house on Everton Valley had glazed pillars and ornate glazed tiles on its frontage. In 1892, the registered owner was the Earl of Derby, whose seat was at Knowsley Hall. Behind the pub you can see the Lyric Super Cinema, which was a cinema between 1922 and 1925; prior to this it was the Lyric Theatre. In 1925, it re-opened as a theatre again, only to close in 1932.

This photograph shows County Road, Walton; another busy road full of shops. The Walton area is also home to Stanley Park, on either side of which stand the city's two Football Clubs, Liverpool and Everton. As well as having traditionally been a shopping area, Walton and Anfield – where Liverpool FC's ground is situated – is also an extremely densely populated housing area.

Walton Lane is seen here on 12 July 1956. Walton Lane railway station was just to the right of the bridge; it closed to passengers in 1948 and closed completely in 1964. The line, however, continued to be used for goods trains.

An unusual photograph showing a Corporation worker removing cobble glaze in Browside in 1951. Cobblestones were largely replaced by quarried granite setts in the nineteenth century. Cobblestoned and setted streets gradually gave way to macadam roads, then tarmac, and, finally, to asphalt at the beginning of the twentieth century.

Kitty Wilkinson's influence forced the authorities to acknowledge the need for access to clean water for washing people and clothes in the fight against disease; she pioneered the public wash house movement, which gave poor people somewhere to clean their clothes. Conditions had improved somewhat by the 1950s, but trips to the wash house were still a regular occurrence, and a washing machine in every home was a long way off.

As can be seen from this 1959 photograph, the Everton area of the city was densely populated at this time. It is difficult today to imagine the conditions that people must have faced living in these properties, with no bathrooms and outside toilets. The photo also shows just how much pre-war property survived the Blitz.

Because the vast amount of old properties in Everton were designated as slum housing, most of the houses in this area were demolished. Here we see Netherfield Road North, numbers 53 to 55 at Rose Vale, in 1953.

Demonstrating the poor state of some of the properties in the area, this Liverpool Records Office photograph shows a house in Everton Terrace following a garage collapse. The Morris Minor that was parked inside the garage is still visible in the ruins.

At the end of West Derby Road and the top of Brunswick Road were two public houses, both called 'Gregsons Well'. They stood almost opposite each other and can be seen in this 1955 photograph.

3

TUEBROOK, OLD SWAN, KENSINGTON AND WAVERTREE

A rivulet flows
Through a place called Tuebrook,
And the Power Station workers
Head home,
And down at the abattoir
Meat is for sale,
That the Wavertree people take home.

An aerial photograph of West Derby Road, with Ogdens tobacco factory in the centre. Ogdens were a major employer in Newcastle, manufacturing cigarettes, pipe tobacco and snuff. Built in 1899, the original head office of Thomas Ogden's factory is still standing on Boundary Lane, though sadly now closed.

Tuebrook, on the other hand, faired rather well in terms of its housing; a large proportion of the original properties still remain to this day. This photograph of Tuebrook in 1955 shows the old police station on the left.

Opposite, above: Tuebrook was a popular shopping district, with high street chains on West Derby Road as well as many smaller businesses, pubs and corner shops. This photograph shows Edward (Ted) Johnson outside the Clifton Arms public house. His daughter, Agnes, ran a general shop on the opposite corner, on Clifton Road East.

Opposite, below: Tuebrook, with Lisburn Lane and Muirhead Avenue running off to the left. The new corporation flats can be seen on Muirhead Avenue. Tuebrook has historic connections with the *Titanic*; Edward John Smith, the Captain of the *Titanic*, lived for a time at 45 Osbourne Road, while Frederick Fleet, the lookout aboard the *Titanic*, was an inmate at the Royal Liverpool Seamans Orphanage, Newsham Park. Finally, the 150lb bell, 900 portholes and all the brass light fittings on the *Titanic* where cast at a foundry in Silverdale Avenue, Tuebrook.

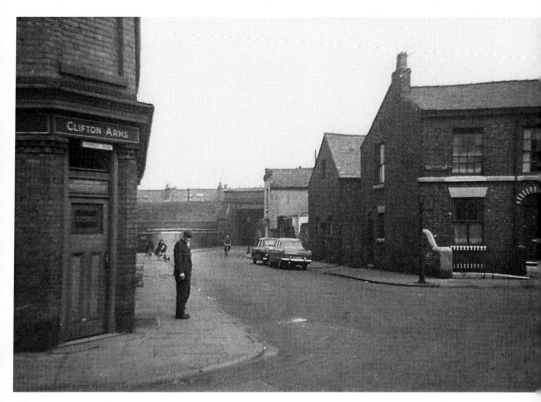

This aerial view shows Stanley Abattoir and Lister Drive Power Station. Stanley Abattoir was the biggest in the north of England and in 1957, when a nationwide outbreak of foot-and-mouth disease reached its peak, the abattoir was closed by Inspectors from the Ministry of Agriculture when eight suspected cases were found in carcasses here. The sudden spate of cases in the mid-1950s was particularly worrying because it took a long time to get the disease under control.

Old Swan was another densely populated area of Liverpool, with mostly terraced housing, but, being within travelling distance of the city centre yet with its own shops and amenities, it was a sought-after place to live. This photograph shows houses in Pemberton Road.

Children living in and around the centre of Liverpool would play in the street outside their house or in the squares within tenements like these in Old Swan. By the 1950s and '60s there were more vehicles on the roads, so 'play streets' were created. Special signs placed by the Corporation warned motorists that the street was closed to motor vehicles. The children here are pictured in Beatrice Street.

Wavertree playground was one of the first purpose-built public playgrounds. It was presented to Liverpool Council in 1895 and, at the time, it was believed to be the largest playground in the world. It had cost £100,000 (equivalent to over £6m today). A stately home called 'The Grange' once stood on 108 acres on the site of the playground, and, when it was demolished, the land was donated anonymously to the City of Liverpool.

The mysterious donor's offer was accepted by Liverpool Council and local people immediately named the new park 'The Mystery'. It was the wish of the donor that it should be used as a playground for children educated in the city's public schools.

Parkland and playgrounds were never under-utilised in 1950s Liverpool – not only did children take advantage of these green spaces, but also adults, who had been starved of the luxury of rest, relaxation and open spaces during the war years.

At number 95 High Street, Wavertree, you will find what was called 'the smallest house in England'. In 1952, the house was incorporated into the Cock and Bottle public house, of which it remains an integral part. It is just 6ft wide, and 14ft from front to back, and was an occupied house until 1925. There are stories of a husband and wife having raised eight children in the house!

The inappropriately named 'Paradise Gardens', which were off Pinnington's Cottages, which themselves were off Wavertree High Street. These properties actually remained until the mid-1960s, before being demolished.

This 1950s image is typical of Liverpool photographer Johnny Lockhart's work. Born in Liverpool in 1922, Johnny was an avid photographer and managed to capture life in Liverpool whilst pursuing his passion for photography and his love of the city.

Just a little further along the road we come to Smithdown Place, seen here on 14 May 1957. Two buses are waiting at Penny Lane roundabout, which would become famous in the 1960s when featured in a song by local group, the Beatles. Although the roundabout is actually in Smithdown Place, it appears on the 'Penny Lane' tourist attraction map as 'the shelter in the middle of the roundabout'.

Smithdown Road, looking toward the city centre in 1950. This was predominantly a shopping area, with terraced housing running off the many streets along its route. It also had pubs, cafés and a cinema, as well as a local hospital, Sefton General.

Cinemas were one of the most popular forms of entertainment in the 1950s as they offered that all important escape from reality, whilst organisations like *Pathé News* provided news and information, as not everyone had a TV set. This is The Grand cinema in Smithdown Road in 1959.

These two youngsters happily pose for the camera of Johnny Lockhart on the steps of a house in Somerton Street, Wavertree, in 1959. Having your photograph taken in the 1950s was still an unusual event, as not many people owned cameras.

The Edge Lane area of Edge Hill, which had large areas of industrial land in the 1950s. It is also home to a labyrinth of underground tunnels, which were built under the direction of businessman Joseph Williamson between the early 1800s and 1840. The tunnels have never disappeared entirely from public consciousness and they were shown on a 1950s Ordnance Survey Map of Edge Hill.

As this 1952 photograph of Earle Road shows, this area of Liverpool was largely residential with its streets of terraced housing and shops, but has also traditionally been an industrial area, mainly because of its close proximity to the Edge Hill junction of the Liverpool and Manchester Railway.

Another photograph of Earle Road, also taken in 1952. The road stretches from Lawrence Road in Wavertree to Tunnel Road in the Edge Hill district. A shopping trip on Earle Road in 1950 was almost sure to get you the items you needed.

This photograph shows Durning Road on the opposite side of the Edge Hill junction in around 1950. The area was still a thriving residential district in the 1950s, as evidenced by this collective of local shops.

A little further toward the city centre is Crown Street, which links the Kensington area at Low Hill in the north with Grove Street in the south of the city. This photograph shows a tram travelling the route. Wavertree and Smithdown Roads were effectively the border between north and south Liverpool.

4

TOXTETH, DINGLE AND AIGBURTH

Captains of Industry
Captains of Ships,
Smart naval uniforms
Gold braid and pips,
A sandstone Cathedral
All here in the south,
Of the city that we all call home.

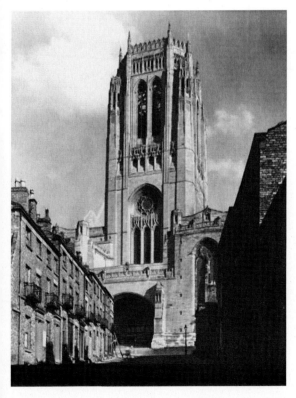

South Liverpool is home to the Anglican Cathedral designed by Sir Giles Gilbert Scott. It is mostly gothic in style and the large tower in the centre of the Cathedral is a well-known feature of the Liverpool skyline. Inside, there are many beautiful stained-glass windows and behind the altar is a large golden carving, showing scenes from the Last Supper and the Crucifixion.

This area of Liverpool also boasts some magnificent houses such as those in Abercromby Square, which was named in commemoration of General Sir Ralph Abercromby, commander of the British Army in Egypt, who was killed at the Battle of Alexandria in 1801. The Square was an opulent area and many past residents were merchants or sea captains, but, by 1950, almost all of the properties in the Square were in the ownership of the University of Liverpool.

South Liverpool contains a myriad of different housing which includes Georgian and Victorian properties, some built for wealthy merchants, as well as the terraced housing found throughout the city. In 1950, the area was populated by people from all walks of life and property around the Sefton Park, Aigburth and Calderstones districts was much sought after.

South Liverpool's black community dates back to at least the 1730s – some black Liverpudlians are able to trace their ancestors in the city back ten generations. Here we see the Cathedral from Hope Street, near Gambier Terrace, looking across St James Mount.

Dingle is the last of the southern inner-city districts of Liverpool; further south are the suburbs. This area in the 1950s was traditionally working class, its housing being mostly terraced, although the area was also used to develop large tenement blocks to fill the ever-increasing need for better housing. Here we see 'The Stone Boat' playground outside the tenements of Mill Street in Dingle.

Construction on the tenements began prior to the Second World War, and many more new properties were built in the 1950s. With the South Docks, the new factories in Speke and Garston, and its close proximity to the city centre, Dingle was a good area to live in. Dingle was also the end of the line for the Liverpool Overhead Railway. Residents of this part of south Liverpool not only used the railway to travel to work but also for trips to the seaside at New Brighton.

There was no shortage of public houses in the city in the 1950s, offering rest and relaxation for many working men. In the 1950s, they remained predominantly male enclaves and, despite austerity, continued a brisk trade. Some were not so fortunate, as this photograph of the aftermath of a fire at Phoenix Inn, Upper Hill Street, shows.

Opposite, above: The Lodge Lane area of the city, not far from Princes Park, is one of the most important Victorian parks in the country. It was designed by Sir Joseph Paxton and was his first commission outside of the gardens of Chatsworth House. The park was the brainchild of Richard Vaughn Yates, a great philanthropist and a Toxteth resident. He financed the building of the park and was instrumental in ensuring that the public had access to most of it from its inception in 1844.

Opposite, below: Upper Warwick Street. No doubt the success of the area's many public houses contributed to the success of Milton's Pawn Shop on Upper Warwick Street, evidenced by the amount of clothing hanging for sale outside the premises; no doubt a few Sunday best suits were lost to their original owners.

Lodge Lane is also the main route into Sefton Park and the popular residential and commercial area that surrounds it. In the 1950s, Lodge Lane was an extremely busy shopping area for the south of the city, with a large array of goods and services on offer – some that could not be bought anywhere else in the city.

5

SEFTON PARK AND OTHER SUBURBAN AREAS

To the park we will go
And the Palm House,
To the lake where the rowing boats glide,
We will play on the swings
Oh what memories it brings,
Of a summer with friends at my side.

At 400 acres, Sefton is one of Liverpool's largest parks; it was purchased by the city from Lord Sefton. The site of the park was once within the boundaries of the Royal Deer Park of Toxteth (which ceased to exist in 1591) and the land then came under the control of the Earl of Sefton. This beautiful snowy scene was photographed by Johnny Lockhart in 1957.

In 1867, Liverpool Council purchased 375 acres (1.52 km) of land for £250,000 from the Earl of Sefton, following which the park was developed as a local community resource. The statue of Christopher Columbus is pictured here outside the magnificent Palm House.

Toxteth, in common with many other areas of the city at the time, was highly populated and, as such, the use of parkland and open space was of paramount importance, not only for children but for adults also. With its lake, Palm House and gardens, it was a beautiful oasis in a busy city.

Sefton Park and Aigburth Road are linked by the beautiful Victorian Lark Lane, which retained many of its original properties. It was also a popular location to live in the 1950s, given its good transport links and close proximity to Toxteth and the city centre.

The Otterspool riverside promenade was officially opened on 7 July 1950. In the 1950s, such an amenity was prized and people came from all over Liverpool and beyond to take advantage of the walks, shelters and landscaping. The park is pictured here at the opening ceremony. The site was extended in the 1950s and '60s to the north and south and an old dock at Otterspool was filled in to make a car park. The promenade offers excellent views across the River Mersey.

The districts of Aigburth, Garston and Speke are all on the banks of the Mersey. Garston is to the south of Liverpool city centre, and separated from Toxteth by Otterspool. Garston and Speke are home to Liverpool Airport and the Bryant & May Match works, photographed here around 1950.

This photograph shows Woolton Road and the Garston Home Guard Social Club, which served the community for many years. One of Garston's famous sons was Ronald Wycherley, better known as the singer Billy Fury. Wycherley fronted his own group in 1955, but simultaneously worked full-time on a tugboat and, later, as a stevedore. He entered and won a talent competition, and by 1958 had started composing his own songs. He released his first hit single, 'Maybe Tomorrow', in 1959.

Liverpool's Housing Committee wanted to provide housing for all working people in the 1950s, and the Speke housing estate to the south-east of Liverpool was one of the most ambitious projects in suburban planning.

Sir Lancelot Keay, Liverpool's City Architect and Director of Housing, was behind this ambitious venture. He wanted to create comfortable housing in spacious surroundings, providing recreation grounds and playgrounds for families.

Over 1,000 prefabricated homes were erected in Belle Vale between 1945 and 1947 in order to provide affordable, rented accommodation for people whose homes were destroyed in bombing raids on the city during the Second World War. One of the largest prefabricated housing communities in the country, these prefabs in Lineside Road, Belle Vale, are pictured here in 1953.

The Mossley Hill and Allerton districts of Liverpool have some magnificent open spaces – amongst them Calderstones Park – but there are also some beautiful houses and tree-lined avenues, such as Mossley Hill Road, photographed here looking towards the parish church.

Opposite, above: As a child I made regular trips to relatives who lived in Woolton and as a result trips to Calderstones Park became a regular and more than welcome part of my visits. Nearby Gateacre became part of the city's metropolitan area and was another prime building site for new properties, many privately built for sale.

Opposite, below: In the 1950s and '60s, large-scale housing developments sprang up in and around Gateacre. The area did, however, retain most of its original buildings and was still a much sought after place to live in the 1950s. This is Rose Brow in Gateacre.

65

Allerton Road and the surrounding area, although more densely populated than neighbouring Woolton and Gateacre, was also a very popular residential address with lots of local shops and amenities on hand. Here we see Allerton Road and Plattaville Road in the 1950s.

The majority of Liverpool's suburbs can be accessed via Queens Drive. Work on Queens Drive, which was to become Liverpool's first ring road, started in 1903 and was completed in 1927. By the 1950s this was one of the city's most important dual carriageways, linking to the docks and cutting a swathe through the suburbs.

Whilst Queens Drive was being built, improvements were made to some of the existing roads that crossed Queens Drive, including Prescot Road, Childwall Road and Townsend Lane. Several new roads were also laid out, including Edge Lane Drive, Walton Hall Avenue, and Menlove Avenue. The roads provided easy access to West Derby Huyton and Norris Green, and the Broadway shopping district, seen here around 1959. These roads also provided a more direct link for transport heading to and from Liverpool Docks and Bootle, and out to Kirkby and its new industries.

Improvement to the city's road network was vital as more people moved out to areas like Croxteth, Fazakerly and the developing Kirkby housing estate. New factories started to open in these districts, providing much-needed local employment. This photograph shows one of the city's first multi-storey block of flats, Coronation Court, which was completed in 1956.

Above: The Kirkby housing estate was a major development to the north-east of Liverpool. This followed recognition in Liverpool that there was a real need for the city to move into new industries, as it mostly relied on the docks. The plan for Kirkby was to develop a new industrial estate, and to build housing for the workers.

Left: Seaforth is at the end of the docks network and borders Crosby, which leads to the popular holiday destinations of Freshfield, Formby and Southport.

This photograph of Crosby Road from the junction with Arthur Street was taken in 1952. The buses shown were operated by the Ribble Bus Company, who served the area from the Skelhorne Street bus station in Liverpool.

6

CORONATION YEAR, 1953

There are flags and bunting
Down every street,
And tables of food
For the children to eat,
With music and laughter
Like we've never seen,
The people are shouting
God Save the Queen!

Rationing was still in force in the 1950s, reminding people that the end of the war wasn't so far away. But in 1953, Liverpool, along with the rest of the nation, cast off economic restraint in the name of the Queen's Coronation: the city centre stores and even the Mersey Tunnel draped their frontages with elaborate displays. Here we see the Town Hall decorated with drapes as the city and its people went to extraordinary lengths to mark the occasion.

The tradition of decorating streets and homes had first become popular with the Coronation of Princess Elizabeth's father, King George VI, back in 1937 and people were happy to revive that same tradition in 1953. These were the Coronation decorations photographed on 1 June 1953 at the top of Bold Street in the city centre.

Even streets that suffered blitz damage were decorated and waste ground left by demolition was landscaped for the occasion. This section of Lord Street, which had suffered heavy bomb damage during the war, has been landscaped and planted with colourful flowers, while the rest of the street has been decorated with bunting. Despite the post-war austerity, the local businesses played their part.

The Lord Mayor and the city coach are photographed here on Castle Street in June 1953. It would have been a real treat for the public to see the coach and the Lord Mayor and all the associated regalia on display as part of the Coronation celebrations.

The city felt it fitting that the Queensway Tunnel was not left out of the celebrations. The tunnel was opened on 18 July 1934 by King George V, and for the Coronation in 1953 the entrance was emblazoned with the floral letters ER, whilst flowers and bunting were placed around the tunnel approach.

St John's Gardens provided a welcome respite for shop and office workers in the city centre; it was a place to go and eat sandwiches at lunchtime and a pleasant area for shoppers to rest in prior to making their journey home from the city. Here we see people relaxing in the gardens at the rear of St George's Hall, surrounded by the banners placed there for the Coronation.

The neoclassical St George's Hall – the foundation stone of which was laid in 1838 to commemorate the Coronation of Queen Victoria – is pictured here in 1953 surrounded by the flags of the Commonwealth and decorated to celebrate the Coronation of the young Queen Elizabeth.

Despite the austerity of the post-war era, the people of Liverpool made the most of this opportunity to celebrate and the shops in the centre of Liverpool were eager to provide the goods. Here, in a brightly decorated Church Street, you could buy food, clothing and all the other bits and pieces needed for a successful street party.

Liverpool was home to the first ever Woolworths store, and the popular Church Street shop celebrated the Coronation by selling a whole range of Coronation souvenirs at affordable prices. It took company window dressers a whole day to complete each window, but the results were stunning. There are still homes in Liverpool today that have items bought from that display.

Liverpool celebrated the Coronation of Queen Elizabeth II in style – from the Town Hall to practically every street in the city – and for the first time since the war the mood in the country was buoyant. The Lord Mayor at the time of the Coronation was William Jones Tristram. This is the view along Castle Street from the Town Hall steps.

A souvenir picture: Her Majesty Queen Elizabeth II and Prince Phillip, Coronation year 1953.

7

LIVERPOOL CITY CENTRE

We'll get on a bus
And go into town,
To the shops and the market
And spend half a crown,
We'll go to the Tatler
For today's matinee,
And get back in time for
Our Ma to make tea.

Despite the austerity years of the 1950s, Liverpool city centre was still a bustling place with lots of houses and tenements on the periphery. There were plenty of small businesses as well as St John's Market, catering for a myriad of shoppers who had been starved of even the smallest luxury, like scented soap, sweets, chocolate and decent stockings for the ladies. The larger department stores catered not only for the well-off but also for those that could afford a little extra. There were cinemas too: the Forum, the Futurist, the Scala, and the Tatler on Church Street. There was the Playhouse and the Empire Theatres. Here we see Church Street, taken from Lord Street.

Church Street is one of Liverpool's main shopping streets and in the 1950s was home to Marks & Spencer and C&A Modes, Woolworths and Coopers, which at the time was Liverpool's high-class delicatessen, selling exotic ground coffee and other luxury food items. The smell of roasting coffee beans permeated the air outside the store, enticing passing shoppers inside.

The C&A store is pictured here in 1955, with F.W. Woolworths to the left. The latter was the first Woolworths store to open in the UK, and began trading on 5 November 1909 as Woolworths threepenny and sixpenny store.

German bombing, however, was still evident as the city continued to replace buildings damaged by enemy action. When developing the site of the Horne Bros Building on Paradise Street and Lord Street, an excavation was carried out which showed what appeared to be timbers from an old footbridge.

Just a few hundred yards from bustling Church Street was Queen Square fruit and vegetable market, where goods from all over the world were traded on a daily basis. James Rimmer (see chapter two) traded regularly from this location.

In nearby Williamson Square a refuse collector is seen at work in the days when the job was a lot more physical than it is now. This was the area around the wholesale fruit market so the refuse collector's work here would have been extremely hard.

The world's first US consulate was located in Paradise Street, seen here with its gilded bald eagle sculpture. Following the Second World War, Liverpool declined in importance as a trading partner with the United States, and the consulate was eventually closed down. Among the last holders of the office were George H. Steuart and John S. Service. The building remained and was employed as a public house for many years.

At the end of Paradise Street stood the Liverpool Sailors' Home, designed by architect John Cunningham. The Home's foundation stone was laid by Prince Albert on 31 July 1846 and it opened in 1850. It was built to provide seafarers with good quality, affordable accommodation, and to protect them from unscrupulous boarding houses. The Sailors' Home was a stone's throw from the docks and the Pier Head.

Pictured here is a commemorative medal struck to celebrate the laying of the foundation stone by His Royal Highness Prince Albert. The inscription reads: 'His RH Prince Albert laid the foundation stone July 31 1846'.

The Albert Dock in Liverpool was designed by engineer and architect Jesse Hartley to take large sailing ships, but by the end of the nineteenth century most cargo was being moved by larger steam ships. This meant that Albert Dock received most goods by barge or road from the more modern docks at Liverpool. It was given Grade II listed building status in 1952.

Jesse Hartley, Albert Dock engineer.

Probably the most iconic and well-known area in Liverpool is its Waterfront and three central buildings – the Royal Liver Building, the Cunard Building and the Port of Liverpool Building. In this photograph we can see the Port of Liverpool Building and, behind it to the right, the White Star Line Shipping Office. It was from the balcony of this office that White Star announced details of the *Titanic* disaster to relatives of those on board, who waited anxiously for news in the street below.

This Johnny Lockhart photograph shows the Royal Liver Building and the Cunard Building, which, together with their sister building the Port of Liverpool, make up Liverpool's 'Three Graces'.

Throughout the 1950s the ferry terminal at the Pier Head was a bustling hive of activity, particularly during the summer months. When the ferry boats were not taking commuters to and from Birkenhead and Seacombe, they were making the regular trips to New Brighton. The photograph shows a packed Mersey Ferry in 1955, bound for New Brighton – a short journey across the river.

During the summer months, the Wirral side of the Mersey was a popular destination for families from Liverpool. After the war years it was a real and affordable treat to take a trip across the Mersey to sit on the beach, go to the outdoor pool, visit the funfair or the Tower Ballroom, and the ferry boats would be packed with travellers.

I remember as a child standing on the floating landing stage, anxiously awaiting the arrival of the ferry; it was a real adventure setting off from Liverpool and watching the Liver Building get further away as you stood on the deck amidst the salt spray and the smell of the river.

Photographed here in 1950 is the Merchant Navy Memorial. In the evenings, the Pier Head would once again be a hive of activity as people returned from their day out to catch a bus home from the Pier Head terminus. The Pier Head remained as the city's bus terminus for many years.

Large areas of the city were destroyed during the May blitz of 1941; practically everything within a quarter mile radius of this statue was flattened, but Queen Victoria's monument remained unscathed, as evidenced by this 1950 photograph.

Above: This image, taken by the City Engineers Department, shows just some of the post-war reconstruction that was taking place in the Derby Square and Lord Street areas. The rebuilding programme produced some fine buildings, many of which still remain to this day.

Left: Blacklers in Great Charlotte Street in the city centre, pictured on the right, was destroyed and had to be completely rebuilt. The company took over multiple small shops in the Bold Street area in an effort to continue trading whilst the new premises were being built. The new store opened on 29 March 1953.

Left: This photograph shows one of the many shops that Blacklers acquired to trade from between 1941 and 1953. This particular shop sold trunks, prams and toys, among other items.

Below: Nearby Ranelagh and Hanover Streets suffered less damage and businesses in these two streets were less affected, although the disruption to trade had been serious. Many of these buildings, photographed in 1953, still remain to this day.

Above: The landmark Lewis's department store fell victim to the Luftwaffe during the May blitz of 1941, when Merseyside endured a relentless week of bombing. The Luftwaffe dropped thousands of tons of high explosives and incendiaries on to the city and Lewis's took a direct hit. This photograph shows the rebuilt store in 1954, before the iconic 'Liverpool Resurgent' statue was placed over the entrance.

Right: The statue 'Liverpool Resurgent' was added in 1957. Designed by Sir Jacob Epstein, it was commissioned by the owners of Lewis's to demonstrate their willingness to rise again despite the attack on them by the Germans. However, with typical Liverpool irreverence, the statue was renamed locally as 'Dickie Lewis', by virtue of its anatomical display.

Left: Another sad casualty of the May blitz of 1941 was the church of St Luke's, which was destroyed by an incendiary bomb on 5 May 1941. The church was gutted during the firebombing but remained standing. The grounds and interior were laid out as gardens in commemoration.

Below: This photograph of Lime Street, showing the station on the left and some of the buildings on St George's Place, was taken in 1957 by the City Engineers Department. These buildings, along with St John's Market, would later be demolished to make way for St John's Precinct.

Above: This early 1950s photograph was taken looking towards St George's Hall from the top of William Brown Street. St George's Hall is on the left, with trams making their way along William Brown Street. At the foot of this street was the entrance to the Queensway Tunnel.

Right: The Town Hall during the Festival of Britain celebrations in 1951. The festival was organised by the government to give Britons a feeling of recovery after the war. There were firework displays on the River Mersey, a procession, performances by Chipperfield's Circus, and a festival of British Sound films.

St George's Hall presented the Story of Liverpool Exhibition and is seen here illuminated from St John's Gardens. St George's Hall has two performance spaces, the main Hall with its Minton Floor and Grand organ and the small Concert Room.

The Royal Court Theatre hosted the Old Vic Theatre Company and the Sadler's Wells' Ballet, with performances of *Henry VIII* and *Sleeping Beauty* respectively. This was an opportunity for the people of Liverpool to see performances by these magnificent London companies.

Liverpool Playhouse Theatre, pictured in the centre of the photograph, was a repertory theatre in Williamson Square and nurtured the early careers of many actors, some of whom went on to achieve national and international fame, including Robert Donat, Michael Redgrave, John Gregson, Patricia Routledge and Sir Anthony Hopkins. In 1951, the company presented *Henry IV* (*Pirendello*) and *The Sun & I* (*Whatmore*).

The Empire Theatre on Lime Street, which hosted the Covent Garden Opera company during the Festival of Britain. This photograph was taken from the steps of St George's Hall and shows the theatre and the North Western Hotel in front of Lime Street Station.

In this photograph, looking down William Brown Street, we can see just how busy the area was – both buses and trams are captured here as well as the entrance to the Queensway Tunnel and the Municipal Buildings in the distance.

Turning the camera around and looking in the other direction we see London Road with the Legs of Mann public house on the right-hand side, opposite Burtons on the corner of Commutation Row, and, a little further up on the right, is the Odeon Cinema. London Road was another of Liverpool city centre's busy shopping streets in the 1950s.

In the city centre we may well be, but in Liverpool we were never far from the tenement blocks the city began building in the 1930s; prosaic and unglamorous they may have been but they were vastly superior to the slum housing that once existed in the streets just behind the fine buildings on William Brown Street. This photograph shows Gerard Gardens. Designed by the architect Sir Lancelot Keay, Director of Housing for Liverpool Corporation, in the 1930s, it was a blueprint for similar housing across the country.

In common with most other large cities, Liverpool has its own commercial district which, coincidently, is centred around the original seven streets, said to have been designed by King John when the borough of Liverpool was founded in 1207. They were Bank Street (now Water Street), Castle Street, Chapel Street, Dale Street, Juggler Street (now High Street), Moor Street (now Tithebarn Street) and Whiteacre Street (now Old Hall Street). This photograph shows Dale Street on 13 March 1955.

Tithebarn Street photographed from Moorfields in December 1954, showing the Exchange railway station. The station was badly damaged during the Second World War and lost a large portion of its roof, which was never rebuilt.

Water Street, originally named Bank Street and one of the original medieval streets, became Water Street around 1540. It runs between Dale Street and the Strand. Many merchants had their homes, businesses and offices here. The impressive Barclays Bank was built next to the Town Hall in 1927 as the head office of Martin's Bank, which incorporated Heywood's Bank. Heywood's was founded by Arthur and Benjamin Heywood, who owned slaving vessels.

This 1953 Coronation photograph taken from Castle Street shows the Town Hall. Built in 1749, it was reconstructed after a fire in 1795 and lavishly decorated. The frieze around the outside, illustrating Liverpool's trading routes, includes lions, crocodiles, elephants and African faces. High Street – one of the city's original seven streets – is on the left.

Left: The Albany courtyard, Old Hall Street. It was built for banker R.C. Naylor as speculative offices between 1856 and 1858, to the designs of J.K. Colling. The Albany is today a Grade II listed building.

Below: This photograph was taken from Lord Street looking along North John Street towards Dale Street. It shows the premises of Boodle & Dunthorne, founded in 1798 when its first shop opened in Liverpool. In 1910, it amalgamated with Wainwrights, owners of another jewellery shop in Liverpool. The business has stayed with the Wainwrights ever since.

A second photograph of North John Street looking across Victoria Street, with the Watson Prickard tailoring shop on the left and the tower of the magnificent Royal Insurance building at the end of the street.

The Royal Insurance building on the corner of North John Street and Dale Street. The design was the result of a competition won by James Francis Doyle. The building is constructed around a steel frame – similar to that used on the Royal Liver Building – and is one of the earliest uses of this technique.

Just a little farther along Dale Street is the Municipal Building, Liverpool Council's presence in the commercial district. It was started in 1860 by John Weightman, and finished by E.R. Robson in 1866. It is still in use today and is the main site for public access to the council.

In 1950, new technology in the form of a telephone switchboard was installed for use at the Municipal Offices, and a photographer from the City Engineers Department was sent along to record the event.

The White Star Line was founded in Liverpool in 1840. The company owned the *Titanic*, and, as a result, Liverpool retains many memorials to the tragedy, including a memorial situated in the Philharmonic Hall dedicated to the orchestra on the *Titanic* who continued playing as the vessel sank. The inscription reads:

THIS TABLET IS DEDICATED TO THE MEMORY
OF W. HARTLEY OF DEWSBURY
-BANDMASTER-
W.T. BRAILEY OF LONDON
R. BRICOUX OF LILLE, FRANCE
J.F. CLARKE OF LIVERPOOL
J.L. HUME OF DUMFRIES
G. KRINS OF LIEGE, BELGIUM
P.C. TAYLOR OF LONDON
J.W. WOODWARD OF HEADINGTON

MEMBERS OF THE BAND ON BOARD
THE 'TITANIC'; THEY BRAVELY
CONTINUED PLAYING TO SOOTHE THE
ANGUISH OF THEIR FELLOW PASSENGERS
UNTIL THE SHIP SANK IN THE DEEP
APRIL 14TH 1912.
COURAGE AND COMPASSION JOINED
MAKE THE HERO AND THE MAN COMPLETE

The courageous conduct of the musicians who went down with the *Titanic* on the night of 14/15 April 1912 will forever be remembered in the Port of Liverpool.

Another memorial to the *Titanic* can be found at Liverpool's Waterfront. The granite monument located in St Nicholas Place was designed by Sir William Goscombe John and constructed around 1916. It stands 14.6m tall and is dedicated to those who died during the sinking of the RMS *Titanic*, as well as the 244 engineers that lost their lives in the disaster as they remained in the ship supplying the stricken liner with electricity and other amenities for as long as possible.

8

LIVERPOOL CITY POLICE

Beneath the statue
They stand and wait,
To meet a friend
Or first time date,
I pass them walking
Down the street,
As I continue
On my beat.

Liverpool City Police was formed in 1836 and became Liverpool and Bootle Constabulary in 1967 following amalgamation with Bootle Borough Police. This photograph shows the main bridewell in Cheapside, Liverpool. All Liverpool police stations with cells were called bridewells. The main bridewell was the central lock-up and was classified as a prison, with its own Governor, who was a Police Chief Inspector. In 1955, Chief Inspector Morris was the Governor. Policing the city of Liverpool in the 1950s was a tough and dangerous job, with officers patrolling mainly on foot, often alone, and with only a whistle with which to summon assistance.

With its own driving school and fleet of vehicles, Liverpool City Police had cars available for both CID and uniformed officers to help them better deal with crime in the city. In this photograph, from around 1959, we see a uniformed officer driving a Riley police vehicle.

The Liverpool City Police Dog Section was formed in 1953 and, when the force training centre was built at Mather Avenue, kennels were also built and a dog section established. During the 1950s, handlers would patrol the city on foot, with special attention being given to the banks moving cash. Although there were two large vehicles to transport them, handlers and their dogs would use buses to get around. This photograph shows Constable Jack Walmsley and police dog Klaus in the 1950s.

Liverpool City Police pioneered the Juvenile Liaison Scheme, appointing plain-clothes officers to work alongside schools, youth clubs and parents to prevent juvenile crime. The 1958 film *Violent Playground*, starring Stanley Baker, Anne Heywood and David McCallum, highlighted the struggle between a Liverpool Juvenile Liaison Officer and a young and dangerous pyromaniac. This photograph shows a Liverpool Juvenile Liaison Officer keeping a watchful eye over a group of youngsters.

Uniformed officers dealt with children on a daily basis, as this photograph of Constable Sammy Robinson helping a little girl in 1954 shows.

In 1948, in order to boost recruitment to Liverpool City Police, the Watch Committee resolved to appoint Police Cadets aged 15 to 18 to the force. So, in 1949, the Liverpool City Police Cadet Force was created. The cadets underwent an initial period of six weeks' training and thereafter worked in the various divisions in different departments, returning to the Police Training Centre for two days each week. After initial training at Bruche, near Warrington, officers would attend a 'Local Procedure' course at the Police Training Centre at Mather Avenue in Liverpool. Here we see senior officers carrying out an inspection of new recruits in 1955.

Once officers had completed their training, they would be posted to various divisions throughout the city. Although policing the city was a difficult job, there were lighter moments, as we see here with a contingent of officers parading for the Coronation in 1953.

The Liverpool City Police Women's Corps was founded in 1947, and women continued to be recruited, providing a valuable contribution to the role of the Police in the city. Here we see a WPC directing traffic in William Brown Street.

Ably supporting the regular police officers were the Liverpool City Police Special Constabulary. After the First World War, the Special Constabulary in Liverpool was placed on a more professional footing and brought in line with the regular force. Unlike the majority of police forces in the UK, the Liverpool Specials had a similar rank structure to the regular force and were posted to Divisions. Here we see Special Constable Ralph Smith on point duty in Castle Street.

Among the many other duties Liverpool City Police performed during the 1950s was traffic control, and as the roads became busier this became an even more essential task. This officer had the memorable task of escorting Liverpool's last tram along Lime Street on 14 September 1957.

9

FUN IN THE 1950s

A bag of jam butties,
Home-made lemonade,
A couple of coppers to spend.
And maybe the ferry,
A trip to the beach,
In the summer
The fun never ends.

Pleasures were simple in the 1950s; children were happy to play in the nearest council playground. Home-made lemonade and a couple of rounds of bread and jam would make an ideal picnic. The summer holidays from school meant that you had to be inventive as money was scarce and didn't allow for many days out.

If you were lucky enough to live within a safe walking distance of a park then a whole day out could be planned. Living near Stanley Park, I would often spend a day there with friends, playing on the swings or paying 3*d* to watch a show on the outdoor stage. Sometimes a band would be playing and other times we just kicked a ball around. These youngsters, captured in a Johnny Lockhart photograph, are enjoying the park on a sunny day.

If you had the money, there was always the opportunity to buy an ice cream or an ice lolly, although the quality of the ice-cream vendors' vehicles was not quite up to the standards of today's vehicles. Often ice cream would be sold from a cool box attached to a three-wheel cycle which the vendor peddled around the streets.

Another popular destination for those that could afford the train or bus fares was Southport. Just outside Liverpool, Freshfield, Formby and Southport are on the coast and offered beaches and sand dunes where children could play. These children were photographed in 1956 enjoying a bottle of lemonade on Freshfield sand hills.

A real treat for youngsters in the 1950s was to be taken to the Pier Head to watch the ferry boats and see some of the other big ships on the river. Liverpool was still a major port at this time and ships like the *Empress of Canada* and other cruise liners were a regular sight on the Mersey. These two youngsters are enjoying the view across the River Mersey.

Photographed in 1955, this little girl enjoys an ice cream in front of the Cunard Building whilst her father, Johnny Lockhart, captures the moment.

Of course the ultimate treat was to catch the ferry to New Brighton, just across the River Mersey; for many children this was the ultimate day out – a chance to play on the beach, visit the fairground, ride the dodgems or enjoy a game of crazy golf.

Above: For children from inner-city areas, the chance to spend a day playing on the beach and making sandcastles was a truly memorable experience. And for those families that had lived through the war, it was a relief to be able to relax at last.

Left: Because of its close proximity to Liverpool, children would often make the journey to New Brighton alone or with friends, catching the ferry home at dusk. I made my first trip alone at the age of 13. My Mother was, however, waiting at the Liverpool landing stage on my return.

Above: One of the highlights was a trip to the fair; the fairground was located around the New Brighton ballroom building, New Brighton Tower. The Tower Ballroom was also a major attraction, with performances by the top bands and performers of the day taking place on a weekly basis.

Right: Another big attraction was New Brighton's outdoor pool. The open-air bathing pool opened in 1934 and was built to competition standards. Between 1949 and 1989, it was also home to the 'Miss New Brighton' contest.

Many children in Liverpool in the 1950s never had a holiday but for those who did it was often at Colomendy. Since 1939, Liverpool schoolchildren had been packing their bags and travelling out to North Wales to visit Colomendy, which was Liverpool City Council's Outdoor Education Centre. The children in this photograph are obviously enjoying their holiday.

In 1959, Liverpool was a city with a bright future; the people had something to look forward to: new housing, new factories and more jobs. Youngsters were able to look to a future without the turmoil of war. Liverpool's music scene was about to explode and put the city on the map forever. These two little boys were unaware of what was to come as they said goodbye to the 1950s and hello to the 'Swinging Sixties'.

ABOUT THE AUTHOR

ROBERT F. EDWARDS was born in Liverpool in the 1950s. He has been a policeman, a publican and a teacher. He is a keen local historian and regularly wrote articles for the *Liverpool Echo* in the early 1980s. He currently maintains and runs a local history blogspot: www.liverpoolpicturebook.blogspot.com, as well as administering Liverpool's local forum 'My Liverpool'.

If you enjoyed this book, you may also be interested in ...

Liverpool's Children in the 1950s
PAMELA RUSSELL

Full of the warmth and excitement of growing up in the 1950s, awakening nostalgia for times that seemed cosy and carefree with families at last enjoying peacetime, this book is packed with the experience of schooldays, playtime, holidays, toys, games, clubs and hobbies conjuring up the genuine atmosphere of a bygone era.

978 0 7524 5901 1

The Liverpool Book of Days
STEVEN HORTON

Featuring a story for every day of the year, this book includes famous historical events alongside less well known and often humorous events from the city's colourful past. Featuring events from as early as 1207 right up to the present day, this fascinating selection is sure to appeal to everyone interested in one of Britain's most historically rich cities.

978 0 7524 7111 2

The Little Red Book of Liverpool FC
DARREN PHILLIPS

The Little Red Book of Liverpool FC is packed with facts, stats, trivia, stories and legends. This book charts the club's history in an intriguing format which will appeal to all fans, young or old, so why not take a look back at what has made this club what it is today? If you want to know the record crowd for a home game, the record appearance holder or longest-serving manager, look no further this is the book you've been waiting for.

978 0 7524 5441 2

Liverpool Ghost Signs
CAROLINE AND PHIL BUNFORD

Take a photographic journey into Liverpool's often overlooked local, craft and advertising history. This book profiles over 150 hand-painted advertising from across the city, investigates the companies that commissioned the signs and is a snapshot of a time that is almost forgotten, but which lives on through the sometimes haunting presence of ghost signs on Liverpool's city streets.

978 0 7524 6570 8

Visit our website and discover thousands of other History Press books.

www.thehistorypress.co.uk